Praise for
Do Unto Earth

"A must-read book for everyone who cares about the future of humanity and our planet."

—**Dr. Ervin Laszlo**, two-time Nobel Peace Prize nominee, recipient of the Goi Peace Prize and International Mandir of Peace Prize, best-selling author of Science and the Akashic Field, founder of the Laszlo Institute of New Paradigm Research and The Club of Budapest, fellow of the World Academy of Art and Science and the International Academy of Philosophy of Science

"A 911 call from Planet Earth herself, *Do Unto Earth* is a potent manifesto for living life today and forward. This book should be required reading in schools. We must act now!"

—**Mary Madeiras**, three-time Emmy-Winning director, screenwriter, Akashic Records practitioner, activist, and author

"*Do Unto Earth* is full of empowering messages and mind-bending assertions that you won't find in science or history textbooks. Given the urgent need for new solutions on this endangered planet, the ideas are worthy of further investigation."

—**Mark Gober**, author of *An End to Upside Down Thinking*, board of directors of the Institute of Noetic Sciences (IONS) and the School of Wholeness and Enlightenment (SoWE)

"From page one, I was hooked! *Do Unto Earth* merges spirituality with our environmental crisis and does it in a way that is as gripping as a blockbuster movie. Brava to Hayes, Borgens . . . and Pax."

—**Temple Hayes**, author, spiritual leader, animal activist, and founder of illli.org

"The channeled Spirit energy Pax states that we are at the 'crossroads of our survival' and offers us bold envisioning and direction. Mother Earth is speaking, and ancient mysteries are revealed! Let's heed and implement these game-changers for the benefit of us all."

—**Sunny Chayes**, social/human rights and environmental activist, feature writer and Chief Strategic Partner for Whole Life Times, and host of ABC's *Solutionary Sundays*

"Timely, high-level and generative wisdom detailing how we may still sustain our beautiful planet while reclaiming our collective and individual sovereignty."

—**Stephan McGuire**, director of Zürich-based NGO Cernunnos Media, Director of Tree Media Foundation

Pax and the Critical Return to Wisdom

Pax and the Critical Return to Wisdom

Volume 2 of Do Unto Earth

Penelope Jean Hayes,
Carole Serene Borgens

Waterside Productions

www.PenelopeJeanHayes.com
www.CaroleSereneBorgens.com
www.PaxWisdom.com

Cover design by:
Andrew Green
Books & Illustration

Printed in the United States of America

First Printing, 2020

ISBN-13: 978-1-951805-05-0 print edition
ISBN-13: 978-1-951805-06-7 ebook edition

Waterside Productions
2055 Oxford Ave
Cardiff, CA 92007
www.waterside.com

For you—
so you know for certain that you are the change and
you have the power

Contents

Introduction

Do *Unto Earth* is an extraordinary conversation intended to quantum leap us forward in our spiritual evolution and journey to enlightenment. This message is not a directive delivered from a thousand feet up; this is a very personal message from and dialogue with the Divine Wisdom Source directly to you and for you. Please accept this gift with eyes clear and wide and open.

Within these pages is the blueprint for environmental repair and peace and unity on Earth, however, this booklet constitutes just one of eight volumes that together make up that blueprint. While we believe that the eight topics, as separated by these volumes, are to be understood as connected to each other and only together give the full message as intended, we also understand some readers prefer to focus on their specific areas of interest—hence these eight mini-books by volumes. (Note: Chapters within this volume are numbered as they originally appeared in the book's full-length version.)

As you begin this journey, you might like to know how this collaboration of writing began.

It is indeed my great joy and honor to communicate with the Spirit Messenger, Pax, channeled by Carole Serene Borgens. From a young age, Carole, a former nurse, diligently studied all things metaphysical. This Spirit Messenger first visited her in the early 1990s when she was new to channeling by automatic writing. When her pen wrote the opening introduction and request for her to be a channel, she recognized the profound responsibility attached and jumped up from her office chair to pace the floor—not easy with three sleeping Irish Wolfhounds covering the carpet. Carole's initial response was to ask if she could think about it and take some time to respond, which she was given. Asking, "Why me?" Spirit responded to her: "You are new to this, you have no bad habits, and you will change none of my words." In time, Carole came to be comfortable with this blessing and so began her journey.

I, too, have been a seeker and spiritualist since my years as a teenaged runaway, and so it is a useful tool at times for me to reach out to a reputable intuitive for deeper guidance. Beginning on the fourth of February 2019, I had several long-distance Spirit channeling sessions with Carole—she was in British Columbia and I was in Florida. I had copious questions for Spirit as I sought further direction for my second title, *Do Unto Earth* (which, incidentally, is also the name of my business), while building upon the message of my first title, *The Magic of Viral Energy*. I was expanding and broadening the message of "viral energy" from personal and interpersonal goals to global concerns facing humanity and Planet Earth. I was also simultaneously establishing the Viral Energy Institute, a learning and research platform for the study of Viralenology.

Through our talks, this Spirit Messenger and I were getting to know each other and Spirit felt my passion for the plight of abused animals and species extinction, as well as my intention to bring awareness to our environmental crisis and to share the impacts of "viral energy masses"—large energetic fields created by both light and heavy intentions and action by communities, populations, industries, governments, and cultural beliefs—on Planet Earth. These disruptive energy masses create massive vibrational pockets of particular energies including love, hate, peace, discord, gratitude, violence, forgiveness, indifference, and compassion.

The Spirit Messenger seemed very interested in this direction and before long, Carole contacted me to say that Spirit wished to offer wisdom to be used by and shared through the Viral Energy Institute regarding this mission of planetary healing.

The writing began on the second of October 2019 when I sent questions to Carole who then channeled Spirit's responses by automatic writing (today, she does this via typing). It was *during* the writing that it became clear to all that this conversation would take book form and adopt the title *Do Unto Earth.*

As the answers were returned from Spirit, Carole and I both had many moments of excitement and more than a few gasps followed by, "Ooooh crikey, this is going to change everything!" The first of such revelations came in Chapter One when I asked the Spirit Messenger (whom self-identified with the moniker

“**Pax**”, meaning peace) to be more specific about who they are. Here was the answer…

> **“We are one with the Universe, not the Universe alone. We are the Divine Universe, yes, and the God being and the greater wisdom, that which knows and supports all and is healing, non-judgmental and tolerant, all-seeing, all-knowing, and Peace.”**

Volume 2

Do Unto Earth
Pax and the Critical
Return to Wisdom

As I walk, as I walk,
The Universe is walking with me.
In beauty it walks before me.
In beauty it walks behind me.
In beauty it walks below me.
In beauty it walks above me.
Beauty is on every side.
As I walk, I walk with Beauty.

Traditional Navajo Prayer

Chapter Four
The Ways

If we had to pick just one anthropogenic issue to funnel our attention, what is the largest threat to our environment and the survival of our planet and life on Earth?

There are numerous current threats to survival of your civilization as it currently exists, but the one overarching situation is the pollution of your environment, poisoning of your water, air, and soil to the extent that even growing healthy food is impossible in some areas. That you have genetically modified crops to suit the wishes of commerce, grow it faster and bigger—what were you thinking? How could you consider there would be no negative reaction, no fallout as a result? How did you think speeding growth of crops and animals in order to sell more and sell faster would be a good thing? We watch your, what you consider good intentions, unravel and destroy, slowly and steadily, your farms, your farm economy, and your planet.

Did you think the spraying of crops with damaging pesticides would spray the crops only? Had you not considered the leaching into the soil and the rivers and streams of this poison? Did you not realize all streams, well almost, lead to the ocean, and the fish resource affected along the way is yet another calamity and catastrophe of environmental destruction? It is a deafening silence we hear from those corners of commerce where money is all-important and the talk of healthy maintenance and care for the soil and water and air is non-existent. For shame people, this is the path to destruction.

Many people, including our scientific community, say that climate change is the biggest and most pressing issue threatening our planet. In 2020, our scientists released a report pertaining to the rising sea level from melting glaciers and polar icecaps. The report stated that one hundred and fifty million people in their current locations would live below the permanent high tide line by the year 2050. May you please compare the urgency regarding the rate of planetary destruction due to pollution versus climate change?

There is no separation between pollution and climate change as the former is a causative factor of the latter. One aggravates the other, therefore, to reduce pollution contributes to reduction in rate of climate change—balance is needed. Your Earth is out of balance.

I suppose we need only look at the example of the extreme air and water pollution in Delhi, India to know that pollution is the quickest murderer of our planet and life here. Air pollution alone kills one and a half million people each year in India.

When you speak of pollution, we consider that of all resources both above ground and below: the soil and water and the air. What is done underground by the oil and gas industry is a contributor to instability also. Mother Earth shudders at the intrusion.

Yes, we tend to forget about what's happening underground, especially as there is so much pollution visible above ground and in the oceans.

As for climate change, is there a way to reverse it? Or, is there a way for us to invent technology to artificially re-cool the Earth?

Not more technology needed and no "reversing" of climate change. Lowering your ceiling and elevating your temperature—a nasty combination.

This was called "global warming". Now this term is not widely used.

Yes, because for many people, Global Warming sounded too scary, so the term was marketed-up and re-scripted to Climate Change.

What is required is to stop climate change and global warming by changing the ways of your industrial nations. Look at the air and water pollution—what are you thinking, people, that you continue to pour waste and off-products into air and water? We look at this in wonder. As you are a throw-away society this takes it too far as you are leading to the need to throw away your planet. Where does it end? Who begins the fight to overcome corporate greed? Why is there no adoption of cleaner methods of heating and propulsion of vehicles in a large scale? Is it because these methods are not widely enough available? And if so, is this protection of big industry and its profits?

This is a sadness and you should—those of you who can—speak loudly for change. If you choose to not do so then you should be ashamed as you contribute as surely as if you made the rules.

When people unite in a cause, change happens, and you know this. Is it time to cease your silence and speak your truth? Mother Earth weeps.

It is time to become a megaphone for Earth and her animals and plants.

Data can vary by source; however, I'll try to pull together an overview of known environmental statistics. In order of greatest threat, the countries with the most CO_2 emissions today are: China, USA, India, Russia, and Japan. These countries' astronomical CO_2 outputs can be tied to automobile output, methane produced by cattle livestock, and large populations that either consume or manufacture products.

On another list that includes a number of pollution sources, the following nations are among those that have been cited as the highest polluters as it relates to the sum total of CO_2 emissions, non-recycled waste, chemical and garbage dumping into the oceans, and air toxins from dirty manufacturing: Mongolia, Afghanistan, Bangladesh, India, Pakistan, Kuwait, Nepal, Myanmar, Ghana, Lebanon. These nations have varied realities: some are over-populated, others are war-torn, and a few are under-developed countries where it could be that people are most concerned with daily survival over environmental degradation.

Now that we have a little context, I'd like to address the argument by some that the environment should not be considered above things like the need to stabilize geo-politics and growth in the job market and the economy. No matter how much we preach about the environment and how much Mother Earth weeps, there are many people in the world who are just trying to get by month-to-month or day-to-day. The environmental crisis might not be the issue that people vote on for their political leaders, and it might not be top-of-mind if they don't have adequate food to eat or if they can't pay their rent.

May you please speak to how we survive these daily needs and at the same time change our ways and methods while looking for alternative fuel and food sources?

Inclusivity is the way. To not assume that people in need of support in food and shelter, jobs, and inexpensive goods do not care about the fact that pollution is making them ill—that clean food and water may not be available to them and their children—is the beginning. All people care about their own and their family needs. Teaching the ways to reuse and recycle, for example, teaching the ways of sourcing locally, teaching how growing their own foods, if possible, are more easily done than believed; all these incentives make people feel they are a part of the solution and not part of the problem. It is empowering to people who may be in need, to know they have tools to circumvent their previous ways of living to become more healthy for themselves and their planet. There is a certain amount of pride in learning new ways of preserving Earth wellness and being able to teach their children the ways—it is empowering. This is how to include and expand the soldiers for healthy living and healthy planet. It is to respect all people for having integrity and concern for their Mother Earth's future wellness.

While we know the world must change slowly, one brick at a time is how we build, and one idea at a time is how we change. Throughout this process there are leaders who speak of the necessity of change, but do they describe the route or lead the way? That is needed.

Now we ask for those in the know to participate and contribute to this change. Those who move forward in their thinking are responsible for educating those who do not.

Pax, earlier, when I asked how we can heal our planet, you pointed to our First Nations people and said, "The ways of your aboriginal peoples, this is how your Planet Earth does best," and so let's get right into this and more.

You should know that repair is possible when your world leaders lead and listen to your environmental scholars who are prepared to lead in their way. This must be a combined effort to teach and inspire and act responsibly with wisdom and intention. Speak to the First Nations peoples on the planet—they got it right the first time and kept it well until interference from those determined to take away their lands and culture. When you look closely at history, you see the decline in environmental wellness began when First Nations peoples were removed from their lands, their cultures were stolen, their language was outlawed, and they were considered savages and not worthy of integration into white society. Those guilty of these atrocities now need apologize and ask for leadership to repair the resultant decimation of Earth's resources.

We are here to speak of the times when mankind felt it necessary to begin projects one at a time and do a good job. Why is it now that mankind feels that all work must be accomplished in record time and quality suffers? Materials are poor and workmanship generally is below quality also. It is our belief that the times of old were when items were made with care and concern in the knowledge that they would last generations and that was the intention.

You have become a throwaway society, and this is wasteful and foolish and harms Mother Earth with landfill excesses. Would it not be prudent to return to the old ways of using high-quality materials and taking pride in workmanship?

Yes, it would.

It is our belief that by returning to the ways of old where community was self-sustaining, you will receive the best you can. To support an artisan in your area, your neighborhood or village, supports the whole village or city and keeps economy buoyant. Not to order from foreign countries where the workers are poorly paid and with no benefits or concern for their welfare other than that they can produce. This is not the way of the future.

As consumers, we need to remember that each and every purchase is a vote for something that we support. We have much more power in the solutions than we own up to.

Again, we say look to the past for the way of the future. Locally made, locally grown, locally raised—this is how you support your future and find the best for your family in terms of food, clothing and more. This also requires little fuel for transport. Know that the Earth's situation is bad enough now without continuing to demand apples to a country where they are not in season.

Do as was done in past times: eat seasonally available produce. How simple. Or preserve the produce so it is available off-season. Generations past preserved all they could, and it got them through. Teach your children and your coworkers and your family members that this is the thing to do.

You need a shift in thinking now. And, it has come to the time that we request you focus on what it will take to move you from such a wasteful society to one which takes care in all areas of sustaining itself.

Looking within we say you will find the wisdom to know that this is the case and begin to work towards re-educating yourself and your families to learn the ways of your forefathers and grandmothers. It will be the best thing you do.

Mother Earth thanks you for taking the next step. You each can do your part for the world.

And, we thank Mother Earth for her patience.

It will be raised by some people that there was warring between many indigenous tribes and histories of great conflict and brutality.

It is the case that in generations ago time, in First Nations peoples' society, there was warring and protection of land, and there was upset and genocide at the hands of white invaders, but when left to their own worlds, these first peoples lived idyllic lives. Culture based on respect for all life, respect for Mother Earth, respect for Elders, respect for traditions; these are the cornerstones of peaceful life.

Yes, First Nations peoples' history was "genocide at the hands of white invaders". This is true and no one could successfully challenge this statement. Yet, I do want to touch on "white" as the descriptor of the invaders throughout history. Was it always the case that "white" people decimated the indigenous peoples? I feel like we might get some push back on using the term "white" people to represent many nations of people over many years. But, I'm not into sugarcoating so if that's the best way to phrase this, then we're good.

The term, which is currently acceptable, is "settlers". It was white settlers in North America and others in different locations. Ultimately, their actions toward indigenous people were similar and the end result was not assimilation, but annihilation; or at least intolerance, persecution, and non-acceptance.

Shameful.

As we seek to emulate the wisdom of First Nations people, are you referring also to the way that they procured medicine from plants, or their spiritual rituals, or the way in which they related to the land as guardians rather than owners of it?

We say to research these ways of the elders and their peoples, touch on the practices that surrounded their community, their society, agricultural and ceremonial practices, and see a time and place where responsible stewardship of resources was the way. Managing resources was a part of their nature—there was no over-fishing or stripping away of topsoil or clear-cutting of forests or wholesale slaughter of animals. Everything taken from Mother Earth was done with respect, prayer, and thanks.

The First Nations people have been the best stewards of your planetary resources, and always will be. They should be consulted, listened to, and included in decisions of world import.

Earth's First Nations peoples live by the belief that they belong to the land and are not owners of the land. If we all lived this way, our environment would be healthy and resources would be available with a healthy balance in place. This perspective shift makes a great difference in all other practices and ways to respect Earth, however, is it likely that we could return to this way of life and release ownership rights?

The First Nations indigenous peoples knew they belonged to the land, yes, but their extended belief was that they were caretakers of the land only; it did not belong to them. They acted in ways to ensure continuation of resources, ensuring they planted and harvested only what they needed, left the soils to fallow and restore nutrients for a later planting. They took only the meat and fish needed to clothe and feed themselves for the season, and respected the spirits of those they took. There was reverence for the land, and this translated into all they did. Under their stewardship the land was healthy and prospered, therefore so did the people who relied upon the land and resources for their wellness. Plant medicine was a part of the cultures and knowing and growing those specimens needed for healing was a large part of their lives. To know that their soils were pure, as was their water, enabled them to live well and long. They also knew that to walk softly and leave no footprints was how to respect Mother Earth.

You know, Pax, First Nations peoples can be wary of outsiders; they are protective, especially of their Elders, and guard them against people unknown to them.

We can learn from the many already published books and writings by First Nations leaders of the past and today, however I wonder: is your message that we should seek firsthand and current voices in those communities?

This will become apparent as time goes on. No in-person visit of less than many days would gain you the information you seek or the understanding.

To not seek them out but to read their writings is the way. Listen to their teachings, observe their culture, and accept that their ways of today are filtered and distilled as their life on the land isn't what it once was. Their current ways have been adapted for today's cultures.

The ways of the Grandmothers are what we speak of and that is what they teach. It is written for all to read and learn.

Mankind is quick to point out the need for care now with the ecosystems. What is really needed is the protection from all levels of government, working together to ensure survival. Much money is spent on studies when it need only be directed to those who know to implement solutions. Not the scholars alone, but the elders of your civilization, the elders of each tribe of people on the planet, those who retain both the knowledge and the caring to make the difference.

Many are those who believe that the Earth will find its way back to full function—to health—this is not the case. The time is now to examine your collective consciousness and determine if there is sufficient care and concern among you for the plight of the planet.

As you observe the change of balance in the native indigenous communities and see the wisdom of the people extend to the bringing of higher education to the children, you can know that the past will rise again. History repeats itself and you are to watch for the resurgence of power in the First Nations peoples. When they reclaim their rightful place as stewards of the planet, there will be a gradual and harmonious return to wellness in your world. It is not too late.

(This will be a real David and Goliath story.)

Returning to the ways of the Elders and their Elders and generations before them in aboriginal society will show the wisdom to emulate for a healthier society today. It is the case that protecting and revering the land and caring for one another, knowing the plants for their wisdom and healing properties, learning of and emulating the wisdoms of Earth's animals—all these contribute to a society of peace and wisdom.

Whoa, this is a sentence to expand on please: "Learning of and emulating the wisdoms of Earth's animals." May you tell us more about the wisdoms of Earth's animals? (Many people don't imagine that animals have "wisdom" let alone basic feelings and emotions.)

Yes, and this is unfortunate. In the wild, Earth's animals, until some were hunted to extinction, knew how to survive on their own. Finding food, dealing with weather, changing landscapes and climate, all were managed through their ability to read their environment. Intuiting danger, sourcing water, protecting each other from predators and finding their place in the food chain—all was managed through innate wisdom of their land home. Family herds and moving throughout territories had boundaries, which they recognized and functioned within. Food sources were rationed, hunting instincts learned, protection of youth and Elders, migration strategies, all were learned and taught and abided by in order to survive and thrive. Pack leaders were respected and followed to ensure safety of the herd.

This is animal wisdom.

As we speak of animal wisdom, elephants stand out to me as beings in need of some special attention and awareness from us.

The gentle nature of this animal is a lesson for all, along with the family loyalty and protection of elders and the young as exhibited daily in their lives.

That they have a purpose and a pattern and a sense of peace while going about their daily habits. Not looking for trouble or threatening, despite their size, is another lesson.

Despite the locals advising against it, an African hotel was built directly on the path the elephant population walked to access their favorite fruit trees. The elephants were not angry or troublesome or deterred, and to this day they walk daily through the hotel lobby, in one side and out the other to find their fruit trees where they graze. They then return to their path through the hotel lobby and in this way all life remains peaceful and harmonious in that place.

That *is* a lesson.

And, how can those who care about them better protect elephants from ivory and game-trophy poachers?

> With influx of monetary support to keep watchers over their territories and game preserves.
>
> Laws are in place to prosecute and these augmented by outcry from Earth's people at the atrocity of killing protected creatures like elephants. Public shaming and large monetary penalties along with incarceration could be added. Public ridicule and shaming is high in efficacy.

I like your candor today, Pax. Preach it!

Speaking of public outcry, while it might be there, it's seemingly not very effective. Let's also talk further about the illegal poaching of elephants, rhinoceros, lions, and more across African countries, as well as the slaughter of wild Congo gorillas and over-fishing of white shark in the waters of Africa's southern tip. Many of these species are becoming extinct and some have such low numbers that they can be counted in the two and three digits.

A friend of mine, Eugene Cussons—a native South African conservationist and host of a popular TV show on the network *Animal Planet*—strives to spread the message of the imminent threat of extinction of many African species due to poaching.

The poaching of these animals is in many cases already illegal, and so how is it that this continues with little outcry from the world? (That is, in comparison to the threat of other species' extinction and various environmental issues that get vast amounts of attention.)

Greed rules, and those who sell ivory and other animal parts to China and other countries representing a consistent market will find those in government to protect their actions— 'twas ever thus.

It is time to enforce world laws, or create them, outlawing this practice *globally* and place enforcement tools where they can be used: rules and laws with teeth and severe penalties for allower and allowee. It can be done.

There is so much turmoil in your world that people don't know where to begin, which cause to champion, how to prioritize and define the parts of their monetary income they can direct to their choice and where need is great(est). It is a slippery slope now, on your Earth, and if the planet isn't repaired and sufficiently habitable, how can endangered species survive?

Perhaps the need is equal between saving plants and animals from extinction and creating clean soil, air, and water for them as well as humans. Sometimes the pendulum has swung so far one way it doesn't seem that finding balance will be attainable. There needs to be a division of the causes and when they are spread amongst the supporters, simultaneous healing may begin. The loudest voices will often receive most support, and now with the rising of the youth voices, they may be wise enough to understand that the division of causes among those crusaders stepping forward will be the way.

I have an affinity for dolphins, and I believe that they are wise souls with distinct intention. What is the collective purpose of the dolphin species? I can tell that there is more to dolphins than we know.

Oh yes indeed, there is much more to dolphins than to be circus animals. This is an injustice and a humiliation for them, so don't do it.

These highly intelligent ocean souls have been responsible for saving lives and guiding mariners forever. They know and they show the way home for struggling vessels and they accompany them to their safe harbor. It is the case that without dolphins' intuitive nature and chosen cause to guide and protect, much loss of life over the centuries would have occurred.

For seamen who understand this, their intuitive calling to their Higher Selves for help out of a difficult situation on the oceans brings their dolphin partners whose guidance and sense of calm transmits to the mariners and the safe harbor is found. It is a partnership of old, and like many is a friendship offered but not always accepted by those non-believers.

That's beautiful and profound. Every year in Japan at a single event known as the Taiji Dolphin Drive Hunt, approximately twenty-two thousand dolphins are slaughtered for their meat, or, in some cases, stolen from the sea to be sold to marine parks. This despicable event is even more sickening when we know how dolphins wish to help and guide us. Dolphins should be sacred and revered. We really do, and *have* done throughout history, some very shameful acts.

Let's bring our talk back to First Nations peoples' wisdom.

To learn something from all cultures is advised, however for the purpose of your current thinking and direction, returning to history to see the future is best done with those who, today, function well in their societies, do not go to war, and resolve their differences intellectually.

To consider the First Nations, the aboriginal peoples of various world cultures, all can contribute. Do you see them showing respect to all people and animals, do you see them as a peaceful society treating all as equals on the land? We say these are the societies to be learned from. Those who treat the air and water, the animals, soil, and all peoples with respect are who you may emulate.

Greed and warring are responsible for the decline in quality of life and no civilization that succumbs to these is worthy of study. We speak of corporate and political greed being behind the decimation of natural resources in your world, on your planet, and to your people.

When we think of First Nations peoples, we tend to think of native Australian aboriginals and indigenous peoples of North and South America. Do you wish to speak specifically to the wisdom that we could gain from the ways of the Tibetan society? What about the wisdom to be imparted from today's tribe leaders in some African countries?

Tibetan culture is ancient and wise in healing modalities. Their reliance on the land for wellness continues. Their peaceful nature and intentions and respect for all are a lesson to be taken by all.

African countries are many and varied as are their ways. They have a common thread and that is their need for reliance on themselves for food gathering and production, their need to rely on one another and on their land for sustenance, shelter, and protection. Their resilience and trust in themselves to survive and thrive is strong.

As we endeavor to learn from our many wise First Nations and aboriginal peoples, I think we need a bit of advice: How do we dare ask for help from the First Nations peoples—now that we've screwed it all up and are losing the Earth—when we still haven't made the past right? How can we apologize to the First Nations people and who

should offer the apologies when the settlers that took the land and decimated the peoples are long ago deceased? Current governments will very likely not give back any land. How do we begin to make this right again?

Your indigenous peoples are being compensated: there is the Truth and Reconciliation Act in place which is enacted and being followed. Lands are returned, the "Indian Act" (in Canada) modified, education and funding for it and housing improvements is in place, but not enough yet. The higher education of First Nations youth has led to stronger Bands and wiser Bands, and tables have turned. There is still far to go, but Residential School reparations are made and apologies also by government. Return of language and culture studies contribute to their strength going forward and working together now with Bands to ask their guidance in how to know and follow their past ways of conservation, brings mutual understanding. The wisdom shared will make the difference in your land and resource management practices.

The indigenous peoples are being *somewhat* compensated, yet I would guess that they are not satisfied with how they are negated, cast aside, and not respected and heard, especially when it comes to their efforts to protect the natural environments from oil drilling and water contamination.

You had said, "What is done underground by the oil and gas industry is a contributor to instability also: Mother Earth shudders at the intrusion."

Let's talk about that. Why does Mother Earth shudder at the intrusion of oil excavation? What is going on beneath the surface from a geological and technical description that is hurting Earth?

> Weakening the stability of Earth with fracking and drilling is what is going on beneath the surface. Fill it with holes then expect stability against wind and weather? Not brilliant in the long term. As more and more boreholes are driven, the look of Swiss cheese begins, and we say you understand the stability of that for holding weight above.

The Middle East is known for oil, however, let's discuss oil excavation in North America as this directly involves First Nations peoples.

The Dakota Access Pipeline is some eleven hundred miles long and moves a half million barrels of crude oil per day out of the ground through North Dakota, South Dakota, and Iowa, and terminates in Illinois. This pipeline was built from start to finish in just one year (talk about high-level vested interest; we can't fix road potholes this quickly), and it was highly protested against by many First Nations tribes including the Standing Rock Sioux Tribe whose Standing Rock

Reservation is directly next to the pipeline. They, of course, lost the battle, again.

Let's take a short trip down history lane because this harkens back to 1874 when General Custer's cavalry found gold in the Black Hills, part of the *then* treaty-protected land of the Great Sioux Nation.

The Sioux fought for their land, but then in 1877, the United States Government imposed the "Starve or Sell Bill". Another altercation ensued at a place called Wounded Knee on the twenty-ninth of December 1890, and Custer's Seventh Calvary slaughtered three hundred people from the Sioux (Lakota) Nation.

Now, here we are again. The Dakota Pipeline is the Black Hills Gold of today, and greed wins again. Can you imagine how disempowered The Sioux must feel? I guess that was a rhetorical question because I know that you can.

Those with vested interest don't see an environmental liability with the pipeline. That being said, I think everyone needs to hear it directly from you: Is the pipeline indeed poisoning the water sources for those living on the Standing Rock Reservation who report drinking-water contamination and water shortage?

What do you think? Water is required for the process and much of it. Leaching into the groundwater of spillage and contamination produced in the process is reality.

What is this pipeline's mental and spiritual impact on America's First Nations peoples?

It is one of disappointment, anger, indignation at being disrespected and a constant need to fight for what was theirs and should now be theirs, the ability to manage their own lands and keep peace with the ancestors. This diminishing of their rights as well as their identity goes on around the globe and is a genocide of sorts—the mass destruction of First Nation peoples' rights and sacred beliefs—it is disrespectful and injurious to them emotionally and spiritually. To be considered as unworthy, unimportant and generally of no value: what a place for a noble people to be in your current—and what you *think* of as advanced—world.

More shame on your corporate and governmental groups.

And yet, they're not ashamed, as they should be. Our corporate and government groups will do just about anything to get that "Black Hills Gold" in all forms.

The Trans Mountain pipeline carries crude from the now infamous Alberta Oil Sands all the way west through British Columbia, Canada with a planned—yet highly protested—expansion to bring the black gold to a port at Vancouver, British Columbia to be loaded onto oil tankers and exported to the U.S. and other countries. The humongous increase in oil tankers is said to

be three hundred percent more than current oil tanker traffic in the harbor.

The people of British Columbia and the First Nations peoples anguish over the potential annihilation of their pristine coastline due to the existing (and inevitable future) oil spills from tankers and the resulting impact on the crystal clear water, resident and transient Orca whales, the wild salmon they feed on, and other ocean life.

It seems that oil money always wins.

Pax, we feel like our hands are tied. The people do speak out. Yet, no one and nothing can stop the "black gold barons" and the power of profiteers involved and the ego of those in politics who will benefit through campaign contributions and voter retention by "supporting economic growth". We can sometimes feel hopeless because people in large numbers do stand up and speak out and it gets them nowhere as they are up against macro-economic control. Do you have any advice?

Ah well, it is the way of it now and into your future. That your people allow government and industry to continue fouling your air and water through the locating and drilling for and transport of crude oil, bitumen and the like is preposterous in your day and age with advanced fuels and heating/cooling methods in place.

What does it take for indignation to replace apathy? It has not yet been identified.

We should like to say the inability to breathe easily in your polluted air is generally considered to be a beginning. In your *very* soon time this becomes reality and your people will look around themselves asking, what happened and who did this to us? Reality is harsh and there will be complications in health and wellness for the masses in countries around the world, as there are now, but until those in North America, it seems, are strongly impacted there will not be generalized changing of hearts and minds to adopt means of halting and reversing your climate crisis.

That it takes crisis to get attention is a sadness.

Here's another sadness: not long ago, the Keystone 1 Pipeline in North Dakota leaked nearly four hundred thousand gallons of oil into the ground.

I'm mad, Pax. I understand that the Spirit World can't do the heavy lifting for us; you advise us and give us wisdom when we ask, but we are the boots on the ground and the only ones that can make the difference. And yet, the people *are* trying. The irony here is that the people who protest environmental atrocities are often the same consumers that drive all industry and all demand for such fuels. What I'm saying is that we're *all* consumers of products and therefore we're all part of the problem. So, here we are.

Pax, the big oil players and the petrodollar system will continue just as long as we need oil.

What we really need—and I believe it's the only thing that will stop the madness—is a replacement for crude oil. Do you see the vicious cycle that we're in?

We see and feel the crisis you are in.

We do not see so many faces standing up to make change for Mother Earth, however, as we have previously noted, many of those faces are attached to heads planted firmly in sand.

The seats of power grapple with these as becoming available and spoken of as superior, but the money still goes to and through and sometimes from the fossil fuel providers and those who preach this as superior.

I find it interesting that we refer to Earth as Mother Earth—in the feminine. What is the significance of this and what is the female role as it pertains to healing Mother Earth?

It has always been the female role to be nurturing. Now it remains the female role also of protection and repair of the broken, whether it be spirit or wellness, and it is hers to continue this on a large scale by taking the lead in growing awareness of the need. This need is to reject the present ways of industry involving polluting and creating of items for daily use that cannot be re-used therefore enter your garbage places forever, and teaching that better ways exist if the need for profit can be removed from the equation and those producers see the larger picture of Earth protection surpassing need for profit.

In your time and place you have great technology and the ability to create the means to travel through space, but you cannot extinguish the pollution, fear and hatred, crime and violence in your world today. For shame.

When is it time to go forward in peace and prosperity across the lands? Under the direction of the masculine-will this has not become a reality—the Middle East grows in violence. The time is now for abundance here, but the structure of ruling parties of government must change first—then it will be. As the sun rises in these places, so does the awareness. Women are to develop their personal power and proceed on the path to enlightenment. The future holds for them the wealth of power and enlightenment, which will transfer to their children and their children. The time is now for this.

All around the world the message is the same. The results will be the same in time. You will know the weight of the problem in time and see the future in the feminine ways. We see the future role of women mimicking the past: matriarchal society and respect for tribal elders, beginning with the wise woman who supports her people with her healing and teachings.

The reality is that most of the world leaders at this time are men. What is missing in the balance of this equation?

Today we speak of the inability of a great many men to communicate his wishes in the great wide world. Why are you still warring in the time when you could be speaking your minds and wishes for peace and prosperity in the world?

Men are capable of so much more. Go inward and ask for strength and guidance to find the way. The way is clear if you seek it. Go forward and ask for guidance. It will be there.

Our concern now for men and women against each other is the strength of one and the weakness of the other. Which is which, you ask? They both have strengths and weaknesses, of course, and where one complements the other, strength is realized. Where one duplicates the other, weakness is realized.

We ask, for now, that men and women who are joining forces to overcome the toxicity in your world, unite in the understanding that teamwork is necessary.

International politics are as troublesome now as ever. In the time of the pharaohs were spats and wars and greed and taking of lives. Now it is on such a scale as to be almost irreversible. Almost, we say, as it will indeed be reversed.

Thank God. So, there is hope for change?

Change comes through the forces of nature and will only be slowed, reversed, calmed, and set into motion for the repair of the planet when the leadership from elsewhere is put in place. The peaceful ones show the way—take the hand of wisdom and follow.

When countries are at war, the environment takes a backseat. How do people help the environment when they're still at a loss for peace, freedom, and safety from physical harm?

We are here to say that the impact of wars on the planet now serves to detract from peoples' intention to clean up the environment. It is hard to think this way when bombs are falling and killing is rampant over much of the world. Peace is needed in all areas. A paradigm shift is necessary to accomplish this. At this time, we ask for those not involved in the process of war to involve themselves in the process of peace and greening of the planet.

Young leaders now abound in the area of Earth protection and restoration. Their voices are being heard and their ideas are being taken to heart and preached by the younger generation. Watch these young leaders and hear their voices—they are sent from the heavens to show the way and it is to be heard and respected and understood and followed. No amount of ignoring the feelings of the growing masses of youthful change-makers will do—they are with you now and a role reversal is in place: the young teach the old and show that *they have the wisdom of the elders.* That they are passionate about change is to the benefit of all walking Mother Earth today and those who await their own arrival.

Only through incredible effort from the majority of the population will this movement create the groundswell necessary to impact the planet. Yours is the mentality needed by the many: peaceful and unwilling to be anything but positive. This is the way for your planet. The peaceful warrior is an interesting phenomenon and bears exploration. We ask for you to do this.

The peaceful warrior—I like that. There was a book first published in 1980 titled *Way of the Peaceful Warrior* by Dan Millman. The book is an autobiographical novel wherein the author meets a wise old man names Socrates at a gas station. The author realizes much later that his enlightened guide was a spirit messenger. (A true story, according to the author.)

I see that the Spirit World still likes the term "peaceful warrior" and I do understand your much broader meaning and message here: a model for world peace and harmony.

Indeed, it is so.

What other ways should we be alerted to at this time?

The demise of many species now and in the soon time on Planet Earth forms a part of the Earth's plight topic. When species disappear from the food chain, all heck breaks loose, in your vernacular. The balance is disturbed, disrupted even, and there is no recovery.

It is clear that Mother Earth needs a full complement of animals, as prescribed to be there, and this lesson in print, Penelope, needs that focus. It is all one, really, as one depends on the other. There is a lesson to be learned from the introduction of fourteen wolves back into Yellowstone National Park. Be aware of the before and after of nature in that area as a result of reintroducing a missing species, a missing link in the food-chain and how it impacted and changed everything from plant species, other animal species, and the flow and direction of the river. This is powerful.

I had never heard of this occurrence in America's Yellowstone National Park, so I looked it up:

Beginning in the late 1800s, the wolf was hunted and killed off because they were eating cattle and farmers were suffering financial losses. Without wolves, the elk population grew out of balance. Elk overgrazed the land and decimated plant life including aspen and willow trees, all of which were critical to a range of animals including rabbits, bears, bees, birds, and beavers. When there were no more beaver to create natural dams, fish habitats were upset, and rivers actually flowed in the wrong direction. All of this happened because the environment was missing its apex predator. In 1995, a small number of wolves were reintroduced by scientists and just six years

later, the entire ecosystem was returned to whole: plant life regenerated, bears and beaver returned, and birds flourished.

What a fascinating environmental decline and then repair, all from the removal and then reintroduction of the apex predator to the area.

Pax, may you please point out another geographic area in similar decline to which we have not yet attended or fixed; a place where we can impact a wonderful repair if we reintroduce a species or rectify a similar scenario?

As your planet continues to warm there are plains areas and there are jungle areas in contrast that are in trouble. In Europe central are areas where industry has stripped the soil, and animal populations are long gone. As the water becomes damaged beyond repair, all that had lived in it disappear and that which was fed by it, died. There is stripping of soil and pollution that will remain long after the industry kills the environment.

Areas such as this exist around the globe—man-made disasters they are, and it is for your civilization to decide what to do about it. Most become forgotten places and there is no incentive to repair.

Similar to Yellowstone Park, other areas in North America have been stripped of natural resources due to over-harvesting of what was native to the area.

It is for all of your people to look around themselves and identify these areas, then to determine a plan for repair.

To speak up and speak out on these topics is how the Yellowstone repair began and how those around the globe can be equally approached. One person at a time making a difference—this is the basis for a groundswell of change.

As we learn the ways to heal our planet, what is the best way for us to endeavor planetary re-greening?

Stop the killing of Earth's resources; then begin the healing. To do this in the reverse order is also correct. Without healing by educating the masses about the reality of losing your planet in the soon time, there will be no stopping the killing of air, water, soil, animals, and also people who cannot survive breathing the thick air and drinking the dirty water. Eating produce and meats raised in a dirty environment does not bode well for survival. It is a circle of despair on your planet at this time—see and acknowledge and act to repair, we ask.

A number of our scientists have said that planting billions of trees is the best climate change solution. Is it?

It is, yes. Trees filter and clean the air with their canopies, roots hold and nourish soil in place, leaves drop and fertilize, and bark sheds and feeds soil, as well. To provide habitat for birds and ground-dwellers is a purpose of trees and forests, to provide shelter and food, harmony in nature; it is indeed the need.

As forests are removed for commerce and animal habitat is lost, as deliberate scouring of Earth trees and foliage is repeated, again for commercial purposes (greed), there comes a time of non-recovery and non-reversal of damage accumulated. You are there in the very soon time—be aware and be warned. It is shortsighted at best.

I think that we sometimes wait for someone, some governing body, to tell us what to do. Many think that if the environment was in imminent danger, governments would step in and make systematic and systemic changes. And yet, we eat foods that are actual poisons to our bodies, all the while trusting that if they were bad, they would not be allowed to be sold. As far as the solutions to our problems, many of us leave it to the scientists and assume that someone will come up with the answers.

Look to your conscience, we say. How can you see what is, know *why* it is, yet contribute nothing to stopping the damage done every second of every minute on your planet?

We suggest *conscience* is the place to begin. To ask what footprint you are leaving on the planet, to ask what legacy for your children, this is the question.

Chapter Five

Food?

Here's something that we do to our food every day: microwave. Do microwaves contaminate our food? And, do microwaves contaminate the environment? After all, there's one in nearly every home in "first-world" countries.

Well, it is the case that these *incinerators of food* are risk factors in your world today. Your environment suffers, as do your people, as these gadgets in use so commonly are not safe in the long term. It is a wonder they have not been recalled completely.

There is off-gassing and there is off-threading of waves of energy produced here and where do they go when the door opens?

You must also consider the ramifications of cooking plastics into your food in this process as plastic containers are common—it is a contamination overload and yet accepted as a way of life.

Some are sensitive to this more so than others, but no person should think safety comes with this process. It is a method in use now for many of your years and as the human body becomes weakened more and more by toxins in your environment, this is one integral to daily life and close to home—in the home—and could be removed.

It is a product of your society of immediacy and instant gratification and does no good thing for you, health-wise.

I just unplugged and removed our microwave.

You mentioned plastic. We use plastic for everything. We buy our food from groceries stores and everything comes packaged in plastic. Studies show that more than eighty percent of teenagers have traces of a synthetic chemical called Bisphenol A (BPA) in their bodies. Since the 1950s, BPA was added to plastic to create a tamper-resistant material and was used for many things including food packaging and medical devices. I'm trying to gauge *how* harmful plastic is (with or without BPA) when in contact with food. Are plastics *so* harmful—life-threatening disease makers—that we should immediately purge all plastic food-storage containers and never again buy food packaged in plastic?

Yes, and until manufacturing processes change, it is not a possibility to find all things necessary for life not packaged in plastic.

And, how about slightly different phrasing: if you were me, would you purge all plastic in contact with food, pronto?

Yes, for reasons stated above.

A set of glass food storage containers is going on my online shopping list.

To replace *all* plastic with glass is not workable. To replace plastic with sustainable and naturally occurring product is. We shall speak of this again.

I know we're talking about food, yet given your answer here, I suppose we should rethink plastic that is in direct contact with our bodies, too, such as clothing made from polyester (plastic).

For the highest of evolved beings—albeit, those that still require food to fuel physical bodies—what does food consist of, specifically, and how is food production best accomplished to feed large populations? Pax, you previously told me that a plant-based diet is what we must pursue in order to save our planet. Can you elaborate on this? Is it "wrong" to participate in the wholesale slaughter of animals and the eating of animals? Please tell us the truth because people are so very protective and indignant about what they eat, their very identities are tied to what they consume, and they

will cite the Bible and their culture to absolve the suffering imposed on animals.

Looking to the past to find the future will show that plant-based diets evolved a specific form of human and this changed with an introduction of meat on Planet Earth. Those vanguards of advanced civilizations have come and gone and did leave their traces in the oral history of local inhabitants. They showed advanced (for the time and place) building methods, irrigation and growing methods, and study of stars to name a few. Mention of them can be found throughout early civilizations' drawings.

In advanced civilizations, there is no animal slaughter for the purpose of adding to diet. The cultivation of super plants, whether fruit or vegetable, in clean and nutrient-rich soil preserved by clean and nutrient-rich air and fed by clean and nutrient-rich water, is key. You have far to go but this is the goal. This is the practice in alternate universes on other planets. Trust in this and go accordingly.

Why do people eat meat when a plant-based diet was/is the way of our otherworldly ancestors?

Nomadic civilizations leaned on game hunting for survival as availability of plant sourced foods was not consistent. Survival depended on availability—another human need to adapt.

For full disclosure to you and anyone who reads this, I am vegan; I eat only plants. I say this up front because some might think that I have an agenda, and well, I do indeed deeply wish for mankind to stop eating and harming animals.

For many, meat eating is not just about nutrition, but also about taste and culinary arts, and it is integral to many cultures and traditions. How should we go forward in our food choices while keeping in mind the motivating factors of the environment, humane treatment, cultural traditions, and general wants and needs?

A contributing factor in saving your planetary environment is moderation and balance is found, both in use of soil and grasses, air and water, and what moves up and into the air from both sources. There is no one way—there has never been only one way for any length of time. Balance must be found and maintained. It is not suggesting a vegan diet or lifestyle, but more emphasis on plant protein and less on meat protein. This also serves to bring tolerance to mankind, not all of whom agree on any one way, as you well know. When it is shown that one works in balance with the other, and mutual respect exists for each philosophy, there can begin to be harmony.

What do you mean by "what moves up and into the air from both sources"? I feel like these words are key.

In your current food production, there is off-gassing and smoke, steam, and other side effects of processing, whether vegetable, animal, or mineral. We speak of the balance being found and maintained in cultivation and processing of these resources. Balance in all things is to be a desired goal.

What's just one example of what you see as out of balance in our food production?

For starters, driftnet fisheries are an abomination, a travesty of all that is good and natural and sensible. Lower the net and pull up every living thing within the area? When your lawmakers have the intestinal fortitude necessary to change this policy is when you may begin moving forward in your management. Until then, those who follow this way will have their way, to the decimation of all in their path. Get it together here people and see the light before it is too late!

For now, we say the end is near to the abundance you have come to depend upon. Right the wrongs and begin the replanting, reseeding, and restructuring of your harvesting procedures.

Could a plant-based diet for the world's population be the way to turn around our environmental crisis?

It would not address industry, pollution, corporate greed, or myriads of contributors to the environmental crisis. To have Earth's population become plant-eaters only is a simplistic measure which would take generations to accomplish: it is an ideal result but must be only a fraction of the overall change.

We have spoken of, and will in more depth, the return to ways of your past, including your aboriginal ancestors as being a contributing factor to the return of wellness to your Mother Earth.

Yes, you have.

When factory-farmed animals watch others before them suffer painful deaths in slaughterhouses, is there such a thing as the energy of fear and pain becoming trapped within the animal's flesh? If so, do we ingest these heavy energies when we eat the meat?

It is commonly known that the taste is affected by fear in the process. It is why some processors' methods are advertised as "humane" as the end result is more pleasing to the average person's psyche and taste is altered and more palatable in comparison.

Speaking of the taste of meat, Pax, what do you think of "cell meats"? These are cell-based meats that are being sold now and are "real meat" products grown directly from animal cells without the need to actually raise real animals. The products are grown in lab-factories and taste exactly like animal flesh because they are. While

biologically it is "meat", it was never a body part of a living and breathing animal with a soul. This cell meat provides the same amount of protein as the flesh of the animal, and it tastes the same (for many people it is the taste of meat that they like, although in time, we might lose this need to taste flesh). In addition to zero greenhouse gas emission, no vast land use, and no cruelty or killing of animals, these products are said to be clean in that they are not laced with antibiotics, steroids, and environmental pollutants. It would seem that the downside is that the idea grosses out a lot of people. (I say that eating the animal itself should freak people out, but to each his own.)

What do you say about this cell meat, Pax? Is this a good idea? Is there a downside to it? Is it helpful for our environmental goals? Will this "lab meat" harm our health in any way?

This is a bizarre thought and a failing replacement for traditional meat as it is sourced. There will be scientific intervention to the extent it can be qualified as GMO, and this is to nobody's benefit. It is not a good idea and will take long to master and not have the desired outcome for those presently considering it.

Bad for health is speculative at this point but suffice it to say there is a limited market for this and the outcome is not successful. Those who wish to market this idea as the next best thing will have to be transparent in the overall research and development aspect, the production facilities, and people involved may not have training and insight, skills, and determination to make this organic and certified to the extent those who would use it would wish. Not the best it is shown in time.

Got it. I wonder: why the insistence for eating flesh when plant proteins are cleaner and healthier, and very tasty products are now commonplace?

I know you've already said that we should learn from animal wisdom, however most people believe that we are wiser and more intelligent than animals and that we are to have dominion over them.

Let's cut right to it: are we supposed to have dominion over animals and use them for our needs, or are we supposed to be guardians and stewards to animals and take care of them? And, I don't mean just for our pets, but wild animals and those that we call farmed animals like cows, pigs, and chickens.

How should we be relating to animals?

With respect, as we have previously mentioned. To believe that all things have a soul and treat them accordingly is the way. Whatever the purpose of that animal: companionship, food, or working and service—respect and kindness shown, as it would be to a fellow human, is the acceptable way.

To know that all animals have a soul brings to mind an interesting question: are there "famous

animals" throughout history who were heroes among their kind or in the Animal Kingdom? If so, were they revered in some way similar to the way in which we hold esteem for extraordinarily talented and impactful individuals like German-born theoretical physicist Albert Einstein, Hunkpapa Lakota leader Sitting Bull, American civil rights icon Rosa Parks, or Indian independence advocate Mahatma Gandhi?

In a civilization where *animals had no masters*, perhaps. The closest we say are herd leaders who protect their families and organize them for travel so the old and infirm travel ahead with the young while strong and vibrant follow behind to take care of predators. Elephant families mourn their dead and protect their aged members from harm. Many species of mammals and birds form social and familial bonds and protect one another, so within those groups will be examples of extraordinary leadership.

The animal kingdom is filled with examples of heroics required to just get through a day, and the strength and leadership shown by the alpha members is quite extraordinary. They would say, not so, it is a requirement for continued survival.

Carole once told me about a particular horse named Blackie whom she talked to in her channeling work for animals in emotional pain. Blackie was a racehorse and she wasn't performing at her

best—she was "off"—and so Carole was called in to communicate with her. Blackie told Carole that she knew the fate of other horses that didn't win; they were sent away and had to leave their home. She was afraid and therefore put up a block.

Blackie believed that if she didn't get away from the starting gate in front of the other horses, she could not pass them to win or place. This distressed her and she felt defeated and unable to find courage to push through. Carole spoke to Blackie about her great size, excellent physical condition, and that she had all the attributes necessary to prevail.

They talked of the horses that were claimed after races and left the barn for new racing barns, and that it wasn't what Blackie should focus on as it could be avoided for her.

Finally, Carole asked Blackie if she didn't think she was good enough or capable enough to move beyond her fears and get past or through the field of horses that may have left the starting gate ahead of her. Blackie replied, almost indignantly, saying, "I am a big, strong girl, you know—of course I can!"

Within the week, Carole received a telephone call advising her that Blackie had won her next race.

Pax, may you please validate these feelings that animals have, including feelings of inadequacy, self-consciousness, and low self-esteem?

Anyone on your Earth who works with animals in kindness will know this—it is reality.

All right, so we now know that the acceptable way of living is to treat all animals "with respect and kindness shown as it would be to a fellow human." The fact is that we enslave animals in factory farms, yet it's not acceptable to enslave fellow humans. We eat animals, whether raised for food or hunted for food in the wild, yet it's not acceptable to eat fellow humans. We drown mice in laboratories to test the mental process of depression and the emotional process of giving up, yet it's not acceptable to kill or hurt fellow humans in laboratory tests. We use animals for their fur and skins, yet it's not acceptable to use human skins for furniture and clothing. I'm sure you can see where I'm going with this. This question is a little facetious, but I'm going for it anyway for both effect and more clarity: should we eat people (who are in abundance) as long as we humanly raise them and thank them for their sacrifice? (Pax, I hope you have a thing called irony, as my question is offhand yet also a sincere effort to clearly know the difference, if any, in superiority, pecking order, "use" for, or reverence between mankind and animalkind.)

There have been times, peoples, and cultures on your globe where cannibalism was the way. Was there superiority of any kind in this civilization—yes, but they still consumed their fellow man. There was a time in a race considering themselves superior to all where human skin was used for lampshades and other items, as there were thousands of captive and killed people of a particular religion whose lives were meaningless to this country of people who snuffed out their existence by the thousands.

Where there is conscience there is not this behavior. There is kindness and respect in its place. The eating of animals became a necessity in past civilizations of hunter-gatherers before remaining in one place and cultivating food became their way. Times change but not all norms of civilization change with the times. As the aboriginal people did, taking the life of an animal in the need for sustenance was done with respect and thanks to that animal for providing their life to save the lives of others. Without this, the practice is considered barbaric by many, and some fall away now from this practice in favor of plant-based diets. There will remain both, but the balance is shifting.

As there is not a way to show respect and kindness to our fellow humans by eating them or using their skins for our furniture, I'm going to conclude that the same goes for animals.

By the way, cows raised for food are responsible for twelve percent of manmade greenhouse-gas emissions: more than the entire aviation industry.

Well, there is a beginning now and a slow catching up to this reality. You will identify this need as being based on a combination of reasons. Saving energy in not producing animal-based diets, saving animal suffering, and returning to an agrarian society to save Earth's air, soil, and water from continued contamination of industrialization. You would say, "It's a no-brainer." This is returning to historical ways and bringing Earth back to clean and pure.

Without the added pollutants from processing of animal protein, the environment cleans exponentially. Therefore, to focus in this area makes strides forward in environmental impact. The cultivation of clean plants can be done anywhere on Earth, whereby the raising of food animals cannot. Eliminating the carbon footprint of the latter is a step forward in cleaning and greening.

Chapter Six

Super Plants

I'd like to learn about highly nutritional vegetables, fruits, and plants used for medicine. However, first, we couldn't have a proper conversation about "Super Plants" without discussing the great redwoods of the California coast, perhaps the oldest organisms on Earth.

The redwoods—they're not *just* trees, are they?

Trees they are, yes, and protectors of the land also.

The energy they share and the air they clean, the canopy they provide, and the seasonal shedding and re-seeding offered—these are sacred trees and are to be eternally protected as the old-souls they are.

To feel the vibration of these redwoods, to know the cycles of the Earth while they have been standing, to understand the events they have witnessed and/or felt, all this makes these much more than how many think of trees.

Old-growth forests around the world have been and are being decimated; this is sacrilegious, and you are not to touch these stands of ancient ones. The resources once closely protected and guarded have become pawns for big business and commerce and have been traded for things of no long-term use.

This religious fervor about old-growth trees among some on your planet is well placed and needs to be extended to cover forests around the globe. It is they that filter air of pollutants and so much more.

Reality check people: without these forests, your consideration of cleaning your air will not succeed. In addition, you will have lost the wise-ones. We leave you to consider this description.

Thank you, that is quite a description and a direct directive.

I'd like to know about super plants and how we find them or develop them. Are super plants a technological advancement; plants to be created and grown through concentrated effort and science? Are super plants the way that all plants were before we started soaking crops in fertilizer and pesticide? You know, we now modify genetics to have apples that don't brown for weeks, and strawberries that are enormously super-sized.

The genetically modified growing *must* be reconsidered as a good idea. We say your people are aware of the seeding of illness in your children as a result. Your people must be aware of the percentages now of those who will succumb to common illnesses.

How does this knowledge affect your people going forward?

I hope it has a great impact and that we wake up to what we're doing.

Pax, what are super plants?

In past times, all ailments were cured through the use of plant medicine. Shamans and medicine men and women in society studied all things growing and knew how to apply and combine for maximum results.

We suggest the term "super foods" is what was before pollution came to growing places and genetically modifying crops became popular for reasons of producing more and faster and larger and taking in more money as a result. Clean foods equal clean bodies and minds and renewed health. Where are you to find clean foods now—foods you can trust to be pure? If the soil and water are clean, is the air that surrounds the growing things? There is much to be done to ensure all things contribute to wellness.

"All ailments were cured through the use of plant medicine." Well, I can't tell you how wonderful this is to hear and yet it immediately brings some questions to mind based on my own experience.

I once had a broken spine in my lumbar vertebrae. In 2015, I had a lumbar spinal fusion with

good results, I will add. Could plant medicine have fixed this? Or, before we go further into Super Plants and Plant Medicine, shall we qualify the difference between what are "ailments" versus other mechanical injuries or degenerative fractures, and some other diseases of the body in which plants are perhaps not the cure?

Plant medicine, as used by aboriginal peoples, was powerful and when combined and taken up a step by shamans, could be responsible for higher-level cures. If a bone was broken there was plant medicine to help the repair by reducing inflammation and pain, not directly to repair the break: this would be done mechanically with the added bonus of topical applications of ointments made from plants, and drinks and infusions made from plants.

Everything had a reversal in medicine.

Here's another example, can Crohn's disease be cured through the use of plant medicine? And, can asthma be cured through the use of plant medicine? If so, which plants for each?

These are issues of interest as your current pharmaceuticals are often derivatives of plants, as in these uses. Yes, these irritable bowels and breathing challenges are treated well with plant use—to open the breathing airways by inhaling the plant essence and settling the digestive tract by the chewing of soothing leaves while drinking the tea—these are the simplistic ways. These plants are known to those practicing homeopathic and herbal remedies.

To elaborate on your words, what plant can be used for those with asthma "to open the breathing airways by inhaling the plant essence"?

These are many and varied across your globe and in your forests—eucalyptus and peppermint, sage, and the leaves of nettles and plants dwelling at high altitudes, especially. These have been known, along with others, by your indigenous people throughout their time.

Mother Earth provides you with solutions to all, fixes and cures, building materials, and food and drink. Too much is taken for granted and too little is being appreciated, and we ask for your people to reverse this.

Do you know all the uses of bamboo?

I've been meaning to ask you about the bamboo plant. It grows very fast and some call it "The Miracle Plant". We have a bunch of them growing in our backyard and when I see them, I wonder if we are underutilizing bamboo.

However, in the last couple of decades we've seen many more products being made from bamboo—often a replacement to cotton, silk, or cruel cashmere—such as pillows, sheets, mattresses, and clothing. Bamboo is thermo-regulating and naturally antibacterial. It's also used to make furniture

and wood floors. I understand from our neighbor that the inside of the bamboo shoot is a tasty food similar to heart of palm. And, bamboo plants convert far more carbon to oxygen than do trees. What should our big vision be for bamboo's potential?

This ancient plant is a food source, clothing source, as well as providing uses in building materials and insulation. It is strong and resilient and grows at a rapid rate. Its use is not global yet, although as a decorative plant only it is widespread. As used to build scaffolding in the orient and Asia, as used to build bridges and structures requiring light weight combined with strength and weather resistance, it is popular and inexpensive. Your engineers might consider its use more in the Western world.

Are there other great uses for bamboo that we've missed thus far?

Use of this product's leaf for medicinal is also shown as therapeutic and has attributes for breathing and ease of lung function.

Okay, so the *leaf* of the bamboo plant can be therapeutically used to aid breathing. How is the leaf to be prepared or utilized: should we drink it like tea, or burn it with fire?

Oh no, to dry the leaf too much is to lose the benefit, so partial dry is best, like incense. This is to be imbued with smoke and the vapors open airways. It can cleanse like sage and even more therapeutic benefits come from this use.

Okay, not to burn but to smolder the partially dried leaves. I understand and it makes me think of a therapeutic sauna: placing hot stones on the semi-dry leaves would create a vapor to be inhaled without burning the leaves as with fire.

I'm very interested in your seeds of wisdom and I don't want to miss something big. Is there another plant or plant derivative of which we, the people of Earth, are not yet aware that has extraordinary healing properties?

Many, many plants around the world have not yet been utilized in modern times for the masses. Known to the locals, the aboriginal peoples through time as told from one generation to another, they continue their use for healing in place of chemicals. Together with the magic of traditional healers they sustain populations throughout centuries.

Is there the plantain leaf that has to be explored? Is there the inside of the peel to scrape and utilize? Is there so much more to be told by the elders? Indeed, there is. Is this plantain peel used for pain reduction and swelling? It is, and so much more to develop.

It would be a modern miracle (or an ancient miracle, perhaps) if we could completely stop using and abusing dangerous opioids and instead

figure out how to utilize plantain-power for pain management and inflammation.

To clarify, is it the leaf or the peel of the plantain that holds the medicinal ingredients for pain reduction and swelling?

Inside the peel is magic.

And, how do we use it for pain and inflammation? Do we place the inside of the peel directly on a painful swollen joint, for instance? Do we scrape the inside of the peel and extract oils and make it into a cream? Or, do we dry this inside coating and make it into a tablet or powder?

Well, it may be used internally and externally for best results.

The scraping of the inside of the peel will provide some thick product that can be used to coat the outside of the affected area and it can be improved further by wrapping a warm cloth around the area to hold this in place and relax the area—not hot, just warm. This will enable the body to relax and absorb. Repeat this until no longer necessary.

It may also be ingested as is, a spoon or two, to speed the process.

Magic, it is.

Thanks for the prescription. The plantain peel is very special, indeed.

There are uses for all the components, as is the case in many if not most plants. It is to know the uses and study them, and then apply as alternatives to pharmaceuticals.

All plants have magic properties when used to their intended purposes. As a natural ingredient, singly used, many have the capacity to work miracles and when used in combination with other compatible plants, barks, and berries, become stronger in their abilities to effect change.

It is your Homeopathic practitioners and Naturopathic physicians who train in the use of Mother Nature's offerings and they are the ones bringing forward the healing modalities from past teachings and practices. Look to them for solutions and alternatives to pharmaceuticals.

Is there a plant that can help with Alzheimer's disease? This would be a big help to our people.

Diet change and lifestyle change together prove to reduce the likelihood of this—it is prevention that is important. Now there is a solution to slowing advancement and this is diet considered, and we say the look toward prevention is key. There is much investigation presently underway to determine a path forward.

Is there a plant that can help with kidney disease? And, what plants can help with heart disease and stroke prevention?

The above queries can be reduced to lifestyle change and to look to prevention first is key. Focusing on repair, as many do, is to put the cart before the proverbial horse, yes? And we do not wish to travel in this manner, so we encourage your people to consider how they treat their own bodies as well as that of Mother Earth and her bodies of water, for example. To keep clean and fresh and healthy requires consideration of use—please remember and do so.

We do not wish to be specific about each one of these current dis-eases your people struggle with, but do want to ensure the balance is found between lifestyle and conservation of your Earth wellness. Our focus is on the large picture of Earth being poisoned and, in turn, poisoning her inhabitants. *These diseases you mention are the end result of it.*

Oh, Pax, can I ask you about just one more disease, please? Our scientists (and charitable organizations) have focused a tremendous amount of time and money researching a cure for cancer. Is cancer cured through prevention alone, changing our eating and living habits, and cleaning up our environmental pollutants? Or, is a medical/pharmaceutical cure for cancer a possibility? (Otherwise, what's the point of all the research?) Can you offer any suggestions for a cure/help for cancer?

While the mutating of cells in the human body occurs for many reasons, this disease, cancer, is a result of numerous current-world environmental struggles underway. While your world grows in darkness of pollution and corruption, your people diminish in what they believe is control over their own lives; the damage is underway in the form of what you call stress. When you combine the negativities with the resistance capability, one will easily overcome the other. Localized or generalized cell mutations in human bodies are not only predictable but also preventable.

It is a study in internal dialog and trust and evaluation of personal boundaries that identifies what can be and what will be. There is no personal boundary established that should be ignored or crossed in the name of business, for example, or for the benefit of another when it harms the individual at risk. Too often the crossing of boundaries is allowed without so much as a warming or explanation of the rationale. Giving away personal power (to influence from outside of the person: family, friendship, business, expectations of the all) is the beginning and the ending. It is a travesty, this behavior, and one which your people do not connect with their personal dis-ease. It is time to wake up and smell the common thread in all this—each person controls their own life and should. When this is managed there is health and wellness and happiness.

Sometimes I get a feeling that you want to add something that I haven't asked. Pax, is there anything else that you wish to talk about here?

It is the case that the neurological disease Parkinson's is relative to your environment, did you know this?

It has come down through centuries and becomes more and more powerful and common amongst your population.

The combination of overgrowth of bacteria in your food chain is responsible proportionately, as is the pre-disposition among your people to it—sensitivity, if you will—to the causative nature of these bacteria.

From where do these bacteria originate?

It now is airborne and has originated centuries ago with the soil and an overgrowth of this transmitted to the surface where it ultimately became airborne. Previously it was drawn up and into crops of vegetables and fruits.

How are these bacteria recognized—visually?

The thing is, it is not, and at your time in the cycle of Earth it has become endemic and continues to flourish.

How can it be eradicated?

Cleaning of soils and treatment with neutralizing materials is the way as it is the root cause—the airborne spores will gradually eliminate as a result.

What is that neutralizing material?

Do you understand the physics of propulsion? If so, the use of this in a muted way to spray soils is a beginning. The product is a composition of CO_2 and ammonia, which becomes, when used together, a magnet for the spores and allows for neutralization. It sounds unusual, yes, and together with the intention to affect this cure, will do the job.

Is there a cure for people who *already* have Parkinson's disease?

There is the similar type of cleansing of the soil to be used in the body. It is an alternative to pharmaceuticals and treats the base of the problem with the combination of CO_2 and a derivative of ammonia. Your science can look at this and determine efficacy, but we suggest that the radical notion of this is to be considered, as there is not a present alternative. It is a flushing, if you will, of the body systems to clear and cleanse. There are alternate ways to dose and internally flush—it is up to your medical pioneers in this method to determine.

We suggest that the way forward now is to consider trials and offer those wishing to be subjects of this, the opportunity.

Ammonia: this almost sounds like it could poison the body?

You may think so and it may read this way, but your people of science will look at it with different eyes and understanding.

There are variables, yes, and for them to begin at this place in their thinking and go forward with derivatives is the way.

Thank you very much for this addition. This is remarkable information, especially for a disease that currently has no known cause or cure.

Many of our doctors of today are not trained to practice medicine in the way that you describe or in the way of the medicine men and women of our First Nations peoples. Once educated through the current teachings of our medical schools, most of our doctors never elevate their thinking beyond the pharmaceutical treatment of illness and illness management. Will the medical field as we know it become extinct?

Your medical practices are splintering into specialties and sub-specialties and sub-sub-specialties. This ensures continuation of investigation and treatment to a deeper level than ever before, and is a good thing. This, coupled with the rise of Naturopathic physicians will bring balance to the way people approach their wellness. Picking and choosing pieces from each will bring solutions.

Further, as time goes on and alternative medicine is recognized and covered by your health-care systems, more opportunity exists for the use of natural products and treatments for wellness.

Now that we have learned of a couple of plant superstars—the ancient protectors of Earth and plant heroes for medicine—let's look at the "Super Plants" to which you referred when you first brought up our need to cultivate Super Plants for food. You've been clear that "Super Plant" does not mean bigger, but rather it means pure and highly nutritional as intended by nature.

You will have no "Super Plants" without clean air and soil and water in which to grow them. We have spoken on this and it is a weakening now in your chain that foods do not have nutrient levels of past times due to these pollutants.

We are speaking.

We wish to say the time is now to move the soils of the world through the filters and this will account for the improved yields. We say the farms of the future will do this and all soils will be screened for toxicity; this will bring a totally new way of producing crops. It is now time to consider this change.

Pax, it seems to me that a filter as we know it would sift small pieces of debris in soil, but what kind of filter would screen for toxicity?

Toxicity comes in many forms, and we speak of chemicals that come from dirty air and water and sprays for pesticides. Your science has ways to neutralize these harmful pollutants, but they are no match for what continues to be injected into the equation. Until your air is cleaned of pollution and your waters not fouled with industrial waste, there is no hope for cleaning the soil on a large scale. Technology is in place and will be presented when earth-cleaning has caught up. How to begin this is to begin the shaming of industrial giants responsible for waste and pollution.

Well, I guess this means that "organic" fruits and vegetables are not truly clean and chemical free, but only that the growing soil had no prohibited substances for at least three years prior to harvest. Let's suggest here that our food producers adopt new labeling for organics, such as: Soil Organic; Soil and Air Organic; Soil, Air, and Water Organic.

Once we truly clean the soil, what can we do about the issue of polluted air as we attempt to grow Super Plants?

Without enclosed and custom growing environments with filtered water and naturally fertilized soils, there will not be the level of purity referred to.

Place a roof over clean soil and begin.

About the Author and Channeler

Penelope Jean Hayes is a new consciousness author, television personality, and speaker. She has appeared on-camera hundreds of times as an expert guest on programs including *Dr. Phil*, *ABC News*, as well as international news specials and telecasts. She is the foremost leader in the field of contagious and osmotic energy known as Viralenology, founder of the Viral Energy Institute, and author of the book *The Magic of Viral Energy: An Ancient Key to Happiness, Empowerment, and Purpose.*

Carole Serene Borgens channels Pax, the Divine Wisdom Source. Carole is a former nurse and longtime student of metaphysics. She has been channeling Spirit since the early 1990s when she was chosen by Pax and given the title "Spirit Messenger". Carole continues to write and provide in-person and remote sessions for clients around the globe, and she refers to her gift of channeling as "the greatest blessing in my life."

Of this trio, Pax says, "A good team we three."

www.PaxWisdom.com
www.PenelopeJeanHayes.com
www.CaroleSereneBorgens.com

www.ingramcontent.com/pod-product-compliance
Lightning Source LLC
La Vergne TN
LVHW050940080826
845145LV00004B/1337